Layer
by
Layer

Patricia Hernan Grube

Artwork by
Donald Leo Grube

Donald Leo Grube

Cover and Book Design by
Alice Christine Hughes

Patin Grube

Cover and book design by Alice Christine Hughes
Cover art and illustrations by Donald Leo Grube

Printing by Community Printers, Santa Cruz

Copyright © 2011 Patricia Hernan Grube

Chartreuse Publications
214 Sunset Avenue
Santa Cruz, CA 95060

www.patriciagrube.com

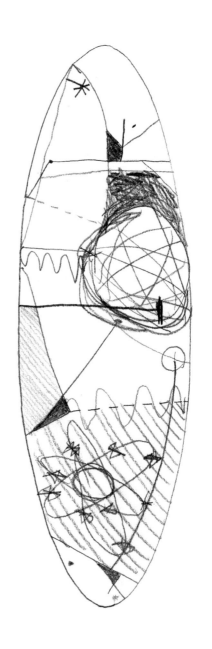

Acknowlegements

My grandmother used to put an egg in the nest of a hen who was ready to begin laying eggs. Thanks, first of all, to those who provided a Nest Egg to make this publication possible. Then big thanks need to go to Alice Hughes and Donald Grube who took on the job of organizing and editing the material. Further thanks to Alice for layout and design and to Donald's inspiring sketches. Ron Hughes and Gail Brenner have searched for flaws.

Thanks, also, to Len Anderson and Poetry Santa Cruz for making Santa Cruz a great environment for poets; and to Joyce Keller for Poet Speak, the inspiring once a month gathering of poets at the library. Thanks to my friends at Actors Theatre, especially those who were fellow Artists in Residence, encouraged in our creativity by Sarah Albertson, Bill Peters and Victoria Rue. There is a group of playwrights who meet regularly (on an irregular schedule) and they are always an encouragement in many ways: Wilma Chandler, Philip Slater, Helene Simpkin Jara, Spike Wong, Steven-Hadlock and others.

For several years, I have met with a group of women poets and I thank them for their tender critiques. I won't mention all who have been with us through the years but here I want to thank Ellie Van Houten, Dore Corder, Barbara Rios, Joyce Johnson and Mary Carr.

I have been blessed by good friends and a supportive family. Some who are gone, have been my greatest inspiration.

dedication

for my family
especially my grandchildren
and soon-to-be-born great grandchildren
perhaps some of these memories will let them know
something of a world
they might never know

Table of Contents

Layer by Layer 3

my century 4

Choosing a Road 6

this morning all the trees 9

After Rain 10

After a Dry Winter 11

Walking After the Storm 12

You Know It's August 13

There Is a Time 14

Indoctrination 15

two pearlettes 16

eye of the beholder 17

Once There Were Sardines 18

My Garden 20

Ambience 21

sunset 22

Dusk 23

At Sundown 24

Law of the Jungle 27

children dance 28

old men plan for war 30

Blue Mug 31

A Question of Faith 32

Jet Streams 35

To Save or Conquer 36

plates shift 37

TV or not TV 38

The Sky is Falling 39

Explosion 40

Every Day 43

it seems as if I'm always waiting 44

Babies to be Freed from Limbo 46

it's time again 48

Finding a Question 51

What do dreams mean? 52

Full Moon 54

Enigma 55

A Loch Ness Monster 56

Dream 57

Whence Cometh My Strength? 58

Jeopardy 60

My Nest 61

Jumping Waves 62

Clutter 63

The Coffee's Hot 64

Visiting the Past 67

At Grandma Gazilda's House 68

Grandpa 70

clouds 71

Mama and Me 72

In The Country 74

Blessing 76

One Night When I Was Five 77

My Tree 78

Christmas (1930) 79

One Night When I Was Ten Years Old 80

Avoirdupois 81

Rumble Seat 82

The Space Between 85

Chicken Soup 86

A Two Mile Walk Along a Cliff of Years 88

Algebra 90

A Learning Curve 92

Values Change 93

Pushing Carriages 94

My mother was washing my back 95

Two Turtles 96

Althea, Nina and Maude 100

we smiled 102

Fashion 105

Lately 106

Creamed Tuna 107

Fulfillment of Desire 108

Sixty Years *109*

Michael and Denise *110*

For Jason *111*

Topsy-turvy Days *112*

I Know His Smile *113*

Walking Along The Cliff *117*

At The Beach *118*

Peter James Hernan, Commander, USN *120*

Stars *122*

memorial *123*

My Mentor *124*

What Can I Say *126*

Singed *128*

Diagnosis *131*

Keeping Alive *132*

The Crown *134*

The Dark Forest *136*

He Danced *138*

Big Dipper *141*

Animal Stories *142*

Bearing Witness *144*

Ndola, Zambia, 1971 . . . . *146*

An Oyster *147*

In China *148*

The Three Gorges Dam *149*

Too foggy for pictures 150

I Saw the Gorges from a Tour Boat 152

The Great Wall. 156

Found Poetry: Acrobats and a Magic Act. 158

Lobby of the Taiwan Hotel, Beijing 160

Remnants 163

The Woman In The Mirror 164

poetry reading 165

Through a Dark Valley 166

In The Shower 167

Sorority 168

one of life's problems 170

Mirror, Mirror on the Wall 171

Cold Feet 172

Poem on Poem 174

Find Meaning Where You Can 175

My Head Is Turning To A Sieve 176

Night Rhymes With Fright 177

Sit. 178

Waiting for Soon 180

our dreams are like ships 183

Finding Light 184

At Dawn 185

there is a tie 186

List of Illustration Dates

October 20, 2011 . . . . *Cover art*

October 13, 1998 . . . . *Front plate*

October 12, 1998 . . . . *1*

Undated *7*

October 10, 1998 . . . . *25*

October 18, 2004 . . . . *33*

November 23, 1998 . . . . *41*

August 9, 2004 . . . . *49*

October 8, 1998 . . . . *65*

October 14, 1998 . . . . *83*

September 10, 2004 . . . . *103*

August 7, 2004 . . . . *115*

October 10, 1998 . . . . *129*

October 28, 1998 . . . . *139*

October 28, 1998 . . . . *161*

October 16, 1998 . . . . *181*

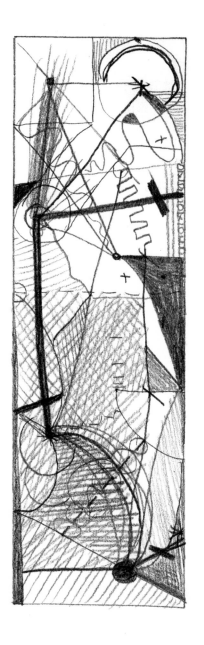

Layer by Layer

Marmalade tastes good on the cake's first layer
then stack it your own way layer by layer

The autumn wind is blowing paper and leaves
and the piles grow higher layer by layer

The roof is still firm on the house on the hill
but paint is flaking off layer by layer

Each scene in a play must be carefully crafted
character, dialogue, layer by layer

Cities are buried under dirt and debris
throughout the centuries layer by layer

Winter rain leeches the soil on the hillsides
and gullies grow deeper layer by layer

Love can be fast and love can be slow
love is best when expressed layer by layer

Faces grow older as wrinkles appear
character changes layer by layer

Eighty years, and more, I can say I believe
living is shedding each layer by layer

September 2006

my century

at birth I fell into
an interesting century
from a time when day was day
and night was night lighted
by the moon and stars
a time with candles lit at twilight
and oil filled lamps
making shadows on the wall

to this time when electricity
lights city streets and windows
of buildings many stories high

from a time of communication
neighbor to neighbor
face to face or letters sent
that might travel many days
to this time when friends
at opposite ends of the earth
or out in space
can chat as if on a porch
on a summer day

who are these children
with electronic blood

this century transformed itself
completely inside out

now that I think about it there have
been other amazing times
what about the before and after
of learning to use tools

what a change that must have been
not just in the way of living
but a different consideration
of life and survival
fear became power

such an opening up
of opportunities
of invention
each one building on the other

when we learned to use
tools our lives were tested
turned upside down
maybe that century was greater than
the recent electronic explosion

what about the century of the wheel

well now you see how this poem
could roll on and on

June, 2010

Choosing a Road

Freeways are great for
getting there, wherever
there might be. They cut
through mountains, cross deserts
and avoid small towns.
Exits are only for food
or lodging, maybe a rest stop
with tables and toilets.

I prefer a road that winds
slowly up a mountain with trees
and shadows on either side
through a valley where there is
an occasional meadow
now and then a field
of new mown hay. Sometimes
I stop in a desert to wonder.

Is speeding through life
really progress? Arriving
at the destination
one has been no where.

I like a road that visits villages
a trip that takes time with ups
and downs, and going around.
I will be rich when I arrive.

September 2006

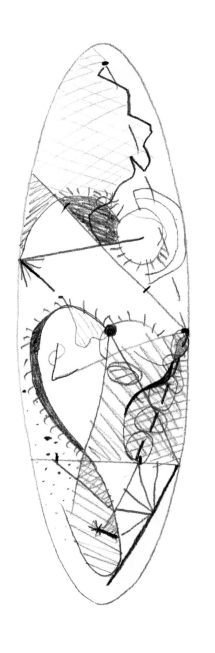

this morning all the trees
are dripping with rain
tears of joy

After Rain

Brown has turned to green.
The field is new with joy
a message of hope
nothing to do with greed
and manipulation.
Grass and weeds mingle together
with a promise of wild flowers
seeds planted by the wind.

Children play in water, sprinklers, pools.
We take running water for granted.

Rain falls everywhere, more or less, with seasonal regularity.
The women of Zambia plant maize in hills to protect the
crop when torrents of water flow through the field. Raindrops
are dear to those who dwell in arid places and they design
devices to hoard the moisture that life requires.

February 2004

After a Dry Winter

Relentless is the right word for rain
this rain, incessant since midnight
but not without mercy
as thirsty fields become deliciously

drunk with water. Dry grass
will soon explode with green.
The banks of the canyon have been
waiting for the quick caress

or deep massage of the river
that will rush to join the incoming tide.
Poppies prepare to bloom and a child
draws pictures on steamy windows.

February 2007

Walking After the Storm

Yellow blossoms on the ice plant open
to the sun. Footprints on sand disappear with tide.
The ocean is deciding whether to maintain
its turbulence. Sun upon the water votes
for calm, waves are saying no, not yet.

Cormorants, huddle on the rocks
to confer. They aren't quite sure.
A few little sprinkles start to fall.
They don't frighten me. I won't turn home
not yet. Dark clouds change to fluffy cotton
shapes of sheep and chickens, rolly poly saints.

Linus, of course, saw biblical scenes
in clouds. Is that Abraham
on the holy mountain? These clouds
are more Genesis than Armageddon.
That was last night when storm, thunder
and lightning were raging round the house.

A sudden brightness now breaks through.
The water begins to calm; cormorants
still huddle on the rocks, undecided.

October 2004

You Know It's August

When the naked ladies bloom
they stand along the highway
into Santa Cruz and
wave to tourists.

Today I saw one peek
above the ground.
It's mid July
and the show

will soon begin.
In the neighborhoods
they will crowd parkways
and sing of life.

July 2007

There Is a Time

I stuffed the naked ladies
into the recycle bin
their pink blossoms faded.
August was their time
a time for barbecues
and family reunions.
Now attention goes
to dahlias and chrysanthemums.
It's time for clam chowder
and corn bread, time
to clean out the closet
to cut dead blossoms
and check the furnace.
A time to hurry roof repairs.
The naked ladies had their day
it's time for them to go
time to get back on schedule
and watch the clouds for early rain.

September 2003

Indoctrination

I started killing although
I didn't want to be a killer.
With one hundred or more
in a pile, I could
sprinkle them with salt
then turn away from
the squirming creatures.

I devised a plan
for death by drowning.
Then, for several days
I threw them in the street
where cars could crush them.
Survivors multiplied
bound on destruction.

Children like to see them
move across the grass
with dignity and grace
their houses on their backs.
So I need to hide my
murderous intentions
as I kill them without shame.

May 2006

two pearlettes

the gardener has worked three days
wind is blowing, iris sways
joy blooms

without weeds, the peace rose thrives
the white cat has many lives
hope looms

a pearlette: three line poem,
syllable count 7, 7, 2
rhyme scheme a, a, b
can be expanded into a sequence
where the third line rhymes in each stanza

April 2005

eye of the beholder

everyday
a resident spider
weaves a veil
over my
driver's side
rear view mirror
very day
i admire the work
and then
whisk it away
this morning
the web stuck
to my fingers
i stopped to wonder
about this neighbor
i thought
about
tenacity
and about
my disregard
of what is truly
a work of art

August 2010

Once There Were Sardines

Screaming seagulls followed boats
riding low with their heavy loads.
Sardines, shining like platinum
slithered from the nets as they
were poured into the troughs.
Boilers kept machinery going
night and day as fish flowed in
to clean and cut and cook
to pack and ship around the world.

Along the bustling front beside the bay
Steinbeck found his stories
about Doc, Lee Chong, the flophouse
and the girls in Dora's bordello.
In a movie Marilyn Monroe
sorted sardines as they moved
their shining way toward silver cans.
That was after she was crowned
Artichoke Queen of Castroville.

Fishing was good, too good;
then nets were empty.
Whistles no longer called
the time to work like angelus bells
that ring the time to pray.

Empty canneries of rusted
corrugated iron, objects of interest
for scavengers and artists, slowly
became restaurants and little shops
filled with tourist gewgaws.

Down the street from Doc's lab
is a world renown aquarium.
The Bay is now a sanctuary.
Once there were sardines.

Novenber 2007

My Garden

The shrubs
are overgrown
and wild
they're beautiful.

Clipped and shaped
they will be neat
and pretty, presentable
and proper, polished, chic
maybe elegant and gracious.

The garden needs to be respectable
but not completely tamed.

July 2007

Ambience

Yesterday the weatherman
predicted sun. Today
the fog hangs heavy
all about the house
my mood is just as gray.

Now the clouds begin
to break and play charades.
I see an upside down ice cream cone
there's an angel flying south
its pink wings slowly fading.

My dark mood begins to lift
as streaks of blue start
to stretch across the sky.

May 2005

sunset

fire sinks into water
water glows
the sun knows
it's only an illusion
in the early morn
light will be reborn

March 2006

Dusk

The sun is flat on the horizon
before it slips over the edge
taking with it shadows
of the day. Birds twitter
good night as they settle
in the trees, their heads
tucked under their wings.
Windows along the street
one by one begin to glow
as inside each, a comedy
or drama is played out.
Lights prolong the day.

December 2002

At Sundown

The cypress tree is full of song
I sip my whiskey, wondering
about the wasted days
and days to come, days
before and days on days.

Suddenly the birds take flight
moving together like a cloud
across the early evening sky.
In the still, from somewhere near
comes a cricket's rhythmic chirp.

September 2003

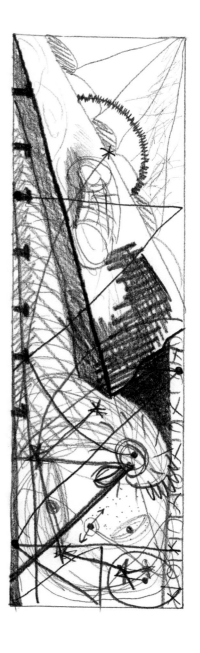

Law of the Jungle

Today on the doorstep
are the remnants of a mouse.
Yesterday a bird.

I'm so annoyed.
And yet the cat was born for that.

May 2005

children dance

innocence and joy
in a world that struggles

activists and pacifists
laborers and jazz musicians
artists mothers
ecologists performers
those who preserve
and those who destroy
look for pieces of truth

letters words lost art
commitment reparation
will courage
belief without proof
a chalice and a flame
coins conflict negation
we meet around a table

eating toil of the fields
hiding behind masks thinking
we have taken them off

innocence and joy
in a world that struggles
activists and pacifists

laborers and jazz musicians
artists mothers
ecologists performers
those who preserve
and those who destroy
look for pieces of truth

letters words lost art
commitment reparation
will courage
belief without proof
a chalice and a flame
coins conflict negation

we meet around a table
eating toil of the fields
hiding behind masks thinking
we have taken them off

September, 2005

old men plan for war
troops are moving to the front
many young men die

Blue Mug

Bombs are falling
hungry people are walking
on a mountain road again
and again, the same road.
A child grins for the camera.

My blue mug is clay
fired in China, specks like rice
imbedded in the glaze.
It is not rice
but chemicals
transformed in the firing.

I drink my tea as I look
at pictures on the TV screen.
Buildings keep falling
over and over again the plane
flies through the tower.

The scenes repeat and
repeat and repeat until
they are just pictures
only pictures.

I drink my tea and feel
the warm clay mug
in my hands.

November, 2001

A Question of Faith

When I had faith, I knew who God was and I had a map to heaven. Sure it looked as though there were a few rocks to climb and rivers to cross. I looked at the lilies of the field and the birds that were singing outside my window. I was confidant that good would defeat evil. Now a man of faith has declared a war in which children are called collateral damage. Young men of faith blow up community markets. They have strong faith in what they believe is the way to heaven, but an evil worm has corrupted their map.

April 2004

Jet Streams

A couple strolls hand in hand
on this path beside the cliffs
a child laughs at jet trails
forming high up in the air.

A faster walker passes me
without a word
an old man smiles.
The waves glisten.

Seagulls find air flows
and soar. Another jet
another long white trail
in the clear blue sky.

As I walk beside the Pacific
I see in my mind
jet streams in the sky
above the streets of Baghdad.

February, 2003

To Save or Conquer

Mission San Antonio is inside
the gates of Fort Hunter Liggett
a mission in the midst
of a military reservation
symbol of peace, symbol of war.

During a retreat I meditated
on the lives and culture
of Salinan Indians who are there
and who were there
before the Spanish priests
soldiers of God who came
to capture souls to save them
saving souls by enslaving bodies
and taking away their culture.
Fields to tend, a chapel to build
the overseer knew
how to make it all work.

      * * *

I always loved the myth, the beauty
of these places, each a day's walk
from the other. Now in this desolate
dry fall with weather both hot and cold
I wonder how about all that lost when
the souls of the Indians were saved.

October 2006

plates shift
chaos in Japan
radiates

TV or not TV

It's raining again and I've developed a relationship with the television. It pretends it cares by presenting potions to heal my supposed afflictions. It tries to convince me that I would be lovable if only I used a new shampoo, if my shape were different or my wrinkles gone. It entices me with fancy wine and gourmet food, with juicy burgers and cool drinks; then says I need ten weeks of intensive exercise.

Some saints had the gift of being in several places at once and this liar in my living room says the same of me. I'm in the crowd in New Hampshire questioning the candidates; I'm at a poetry reading in Berkeley, a party at the Oscars; I'm a friend of Barbara Walters who tells me secrets and Charlie Rose who introduces me to world famous thinkers and celebrities.

My concentration is constantly interrupted. When I'm enthralled by a drama or caught up in a comedy my thoughts are shattered. Just as I focus my attention it breaks in with a loud voice: *Look at me, I want to make you well, make you pretty, make you hungry, make you anxious and dull your ability to think for yourself.* This other in my living room massages my nerves and tells me lies. It demands my time, my money, my thoughts, but never says, *I love you.*

January, 2004

The Sky is Falling

The Little Red Hen poured herself a cup of tea
and opened the window to smell the fresh new day.
At eight o'clock she will listen to the news.
Chicken Little has been replaced by Katie
and Matt. Everyday, regular as clock work
they report that the sky is falling.

When Chicken Little told us
that the sky was falling,
everyone went running to hold up the sky
over this patch of world or that.
Who came to help me plant my wheat?
No one. I sowed the seeds and then
ran after the rest of them
while weeds grew in my wheat.

If Matt and Katie say that the sky is falling
everyone will go off to hold up the sky.
Not me. I'll stay right here and bake my bread.
If I say, *Who will help me eat my bread?*

They all will shout, *We will.*

Then I will say, *Good, we'll eat bread
together and watch the news.
We'll find out if the sky is really falling.*

March 2003

Explosion

An explosion wakes us, broken glass covers the bed, the bureau, the rug and is in the corners of every room. The children are awake and crying. Neighbors gather in the street to ask questions. All our houses have been damaged. It seems as if it is a war.

No fear of war in this quiet town across the hills from the Pacific. One man remembers that during World War II, enemy submarines were seen off shore. Now, here, in this neighborhood a house exploded in the night.

There are ashes on the roses, pieces of a portrait in the peonies. Black and white photos, a piece of a smile, an eye, part of a clapboard house. There's a dog, I mean part of a picture of a dog. The tree fort has fallen, the mud pies are all broken.

February 2004

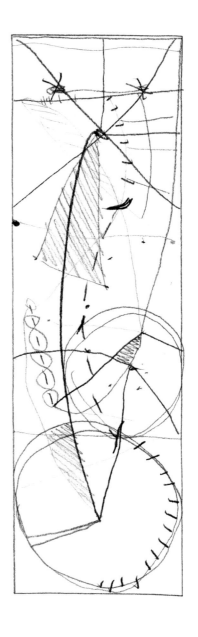

Every Day

I see chairs piled up
in the patio. Every day I plan
to put them in the shed.
Every morning I wake
to see the chairs still there.

They mock me, remind me
of things not done, not finished
not even started. Dreams are
in the planning stage and some
have ended in the shredder.

When I take the last undy
from the drawer, I know
it's time to do some laundry.
As I jot these notes there are
dishes in the sink. It was

too late last night to start
the vacuum cleaner. I'll put
it off until later today and now
I'll make some cookies or
better yet, I'll write a poem.

December 2007

it seems as if I'm always waiting

waiting for the baby to be born
the water for the tea to boil
the water for the birth to break
waiting dinner — then the soufflé falls

it takes an hour
for the bread to rise
nobody knows how long
for the pot to boil

when can I learn to tie my shoes
are we almost there
will it soon be summer
will daddy be home soon
I'll wait for him by the bridge

waiting to start life
with a husband
home from overseas
waiting for the war to end

waiting for rain
then waiting for the rain to stop
for Christmas, for winter to end
for the Christ to rise
for morning to come
for the first star at night

for time to plant seeds
for dreams to come true
waiting for the muse
for the mail
for the phone to ring

was I anxious in the womb
waiting to be born
Mama said that I was late
a month or more
what was I waiting for?

January 2006

Babies to be Freed from Limbo

The Catholic Church appears close
to making a definitive statement
rejecting the concept of limbo.

In the news this month: heaven
is overwhelmed by a tsunami
of babies. Waiting for centuries
they are now free, they run, they crawl
some cuddled in the arms
of good women, born before the Christ.

The terms of the 13th Century
doctrine seem to include
Plato, whose arguments
evidently, did not open
the gates of heaven. He can now
enter into a dialogue with God.

Moses is among the multitudes.
He led his people to the holy land
but was not allowed by Yahweh
to enter there. Evidently
he was not allowed
to enter heaven until now.

What about the children
in missionary lands
our pennies were not enough
to save them all. My young
worries can now be set aside
they have all gone to heaven.

The shadows of limbo
have been dispersed
the gates to heaven open.
What happens next? I wonder
about purgatory. Is it's
existence now in limbo?

... The inhabitants (of Limbo) include Plato, Moses, Abraham and lots of babies. Now after more than 700 years of shadowy existence, limbo faces closure. ... Roman Catholic theologians ... discuss a document which would sweep the concept out of the church's teaching. ... In the 13th century (limbo was) a solution to the theological conundrum of what happened to babies who died before they were christened. According to doctrine, they could not go to heaven because their original sin had not been expunged by baptism. ...They scarcely deserved purgatory, let alone hell. Limbo also proved a useful solution to other problems such as where to put holy people who lived before Christ and who also had no chance of baptism. Dante added the classical sages.
~The Guardian, John Hooper, November 30, 2005

December 2005

it's time again

time again to send best wishes
time again for joy
time to gather strength
to see the season through
time to forgive
time to remember
time to sigh
to catch a breath
a slow deep breath
and count to ten

nights are longer
mornings colder
many the shoppers
many the songs
there are lights on the tree
the house smells like pie
it's time to stop and breathe
it's time to stir up the fire
to sit by the fire
and let the world keep turning

December 2005

Finding a Question

I woke up early with a question
going around and around
in my head. I've always thought
that if I asked a question
I could discover
a direction to explore.

Religions try to have answers
to the big questions of life's
unbearable not knowing.
They fight to defend
their own version of god.

I believe big questions don't
solve problems. Its necessary
to find the little question that
will dig and probe and wiggle
into chaos. However, I am
the proverbial ostrich when
I know the necessity to meet
a situation face to face.

This whole thing is a question
and this question is the answer
to why I couldn't sleep.

October 2007

What do dreams mean?

As clouds, like horizontal pleated shades
ripple up the sky and fade; I feel
a shivering anxiety. Not fear
just a feeling of uncertainty left behind
by a dream that disappeared at dawn.

I am running, running somewhere
running through tall grass. Paths
become dark and narrow alleys
with no escape.

                                    I am running

running past tall buildings where
cold stone faces look down on me.
Then like a scene shift from a movie
I am back in a field, blinded by the sun

                        suddenly I sit up in bed.

Studying the sky I feel a chill.
What could it mean? What do dreams
ever mean? Why did I run?
I try to go in imagination to that field
and lie down in the grass

then I remember

watching *North by Northwest* on
television just before I went to sleep.

It's easy to say that the movie
was the inspiration. And yet somehow

it seems as if

I am running away from finding
the deeper meaning of the dream.

February 2006

Full Moon

Tranquility is a word that tastes
like butter mixed with honey
spread on freshly baked bread.
My pillow is soft, the cool crisp linen
smells like summer.

Let the moon look in my face
and see my secrets. Let it shine
into my soul and burn away
the mold, the moss and negativity.
Then tranquility will warm the room
and soften harsh edges of the day.

It comes without an invitation
creeping into my life like a child
climbing silently into his mother's bed
then goes like a summer shower
leaving behind the fragrance
of damp earth and new mown hay.

January 2003

Enigma

You have a long life habit
of saying, *Sweetheart*
in your casual conversation
which means nothing
in particular.
Being a lonesome
love starved woman
I snatch the word, in spite
of trying desperately
not to fall in love with you.

August 2011

A Loch Ness Monster

Sometimes the monster rises
from deep in my subliminal
            where it hides and sometimes
                                    rumbles.

Suddenly, today
            just as I woke from sleep
                        the monster surfaced

from the lower chambers of my mind
            then dived deep before
                        my eyes could focus.

Am I whipping myself again with strips of guilt.

Not knowing when I need to know.
Not acting when I need to act.
Not wanting to see when I need to see.
Not trying, really trying?
            Now I wonder
                        am I lying to myself again?

September 2008

Dream

No man or beast can hear
my scream. It gains sound only
as it circulates among the stars.
Above the timberline the air
is thin and dry. A rocky path
steep, with many crevices
leads into a dark forest that opens
to a valley where a mountain lake

reflects the morning sky.
Moss is soft on my bare feet.
The water quivers as if a pebble
were thrown by a child. Visions
of my self spread out, each
calls to me, here I am.

In wider and wider circles
they lose each other, and
I pull myself together to go on
but the trail has forked
to many arteries. I look back
to return as I came but there is
only the forest. I turn
and turn again and again
then take a step with care.

September 2003

Whence Cometh My Strength?

Breathe from the abdomen.
Breathe deeper than usual.

Focus on the muscle you want to engage
the trainer says, the abs
the quadriceps, the groin.
Contract the gluteals. Rotate the pelvis
don't forget the hamstrings and the thighs.

Breathe deeper than usual.

I am strong, getting stronger
not strong enough to put things right.
Breathe deeper than usual.
I could suggest but dare not give answers
for questions that have not been asked.

Breathe deeper than usual.

Breathe from the abdomen.
Engage the muscles of the back.
Shoulders, hips, knees
and ankles vertically in line.
The spine will straighten, become flexible.

Breathe deeper than usual.

Tonight I feel like finishing the Canadian.
I keep it in the cupboard underneath the sink.
The world is askew. How can I put things right?

Just one shot will dull the pain.
Did I forget to say that there is pain?

Breathe from the abdomen.
Breathe deeper than usual.

Jeopardy

Answers have questions
but questions do not
always have answers.

My answers
are different
from your answers
to the same questions.

Sometimes our answers
are the same, but
to different questions.

It seems we will never have
the same question
with the same answer.

There are answers
I want to hear
but do not dare
to ask the questions.

December 2010

My Nest

From my window I see a robin bringing yarn
to build a nest. I sit and watch this bird
although my sink is full of dirty dishes
the carpet on the stairs needs cleaning and
in the garden weeds crowd out the daffodils.
The robin chose the thorny bougainvillea
to be a safe place for her fledglings.
My neighbor plans to prune the vines
on Saturday. The nest is doomed.

What is my don't care attitude?
A downward turn in mood is not depression.
The TV tries to sell me drugs with possible
side effects, headaches, bleeding ulcers
sometimes shortness of breath
sometimes no breath at all. I like to think
it's growth. You say that's stretching it.
I say relax, patience will be its own reward
chaos needs time to sort itself out.
The robin will salvage yarn and twine.
She will build again.

February 2003

Jumping Waves

Oh —

What

A great wave

It's tall

Its face shines

Crinkles are

Just beginning

Along the crest

If I catch it right

It will lift me

Up and over

And leave me

To tread deep water

If it breaks too soon

It will turn me and twist me

I will be tasting sand

Here I go . . .

to meet it . . .

I'm . . . up . . . over . . .

and swimming toward the shore

May 2003

Clutter

On the kitchen counter is a little temple
of canned tuna, actually albacore.
I see it now, two weeks since my trip to Costco.

Some peanut shells are hiding behind
an overripe banana, a lemon and two apples.
The fruit bowl, once full, now has come to this.

The high shelf challenges me
so piles of dishes clutter the counter.
This is true. I confess. It seems to be

a metaphor for my lack of order
a yearning for a sense of caring
a need to bring peace into my life.

May 2009

The Coffee's Hot

My plan is to write a poem
about the past and people
who are gone. I don't want
them to be forgotten.

I am distracted by the television
not able to resist the click that invites
the world into my room. Former
and future presidents come in

while I am still in my pajamas.
Even now, as I write, Obama
is seducing me and earlier
Hillary was here for coffee.

She said her hubby would go
wherever she would send him.
There are some who ask, where?
Well, that's a different story.

After such a chat, it's
difficult to start a poem
about a little girl and her
growing up to an ordinary life.

September 2007

Visiting the Past

Images float across my mind
renewing feelings from when
I was a little girl, laughing
playing in places where houses
have now fallen into disrepair
their gardens dry as desert sand.

I took a trip to Arizona to answer
the yearning of a wandering spirit.
In the plaza in Ajo, the town
where I was born, I stood
under arches, watching shadows
stretch across the walk. It's here
I took my first baby steps.

In Phoenix I found a house where
we once lived. The palm trees
have grown tall along the sidewalk
where I would run down the block
looking both ways at the crossing
to find Grandma waiting
holding out her arms to me.

January 2006

At Grandma Gazilda's House

Drapes of rough monk's cloth
were held by heavy rings
on twisted metal rods.
Black daggers at each end
kept everything from sliding off.
Thin lines like spider webs

on the unbleached fabric
made a dramatic background
for the rusty orange and brown
geometric design. My muslin
curtains also slide back
and forth on black metal.

On a bureau, was a sculpture,
probably pewter, of a knight
in full armor. He and his horse
both gleamed like silver, both
at attention, ready for action
sword unsheathed.

Gazilda's carpet was a garden
of flowers with a border that kept
the blossoms where they belonged.
I lay there every afternoon at five
to hear my favorite program
coming to you from radio station
KTAR, atop the Heard Building
in Phoenix Arizona.

I was enthralled by the exploits
of Little Orphan Annie, a girl
of courage and imagination. She
and the knight, both seekers of justice.

Looking back I think that Annie
and Don Quixote have been models
for my life. I have no interest
in Miss Muffet, who was easily
scared by a spider. Although
I did, and still do, like curds and whey.

May 2010

Grandpa

Grandpa used to flirt with every girl
who came into his sight.
We chuckled, thinking it a joke.

He told me once that in his youth
he liked the girl who kicked
her heels the highest.

I thought it strange but then
I learned that it's the style
of Irish dance

and that he yearned
to be a boy again
listening to the fiddler

watching all the girls
to find the one
who kicked her heels the highest.

March 2011

clouds

lying on the grass
looking at clouds
                    how old was I then
                              maybe four, maybe five

no, I couldn't have been five
because this was before
I lived with Grandma Gazilda
so I could go to kindergarten

she and Grandpa lived in a duplex on Oakland Avenue
there was a candy store on Van Buren Boulevard
and after I spent my penny, I would stand on the corner
                                        and watch cars
                              long lines of cars
                    solemnly
          driving toward the cemetery

before that when I was three I also lived with Grandma
          that was when Mama was in the sanatorium

the clouds drift by
                    change shapes
                              soft and comforting

January 2009

Mama and Me

Mama was one for tragedy. When friends would gather and tell stories, she would relate, over and over again, how Daddy upturned my carriage as he was pushing it down a hill. He was afraid to take me out again. I remember tumbling head over heels only because Mama described it so vividly.

She would tell how I was born in the desert in a mining town called Ajo. And of the time I pulled a cloth from the table, spilling hot cocoa in my face. Mama, with presence of mind, wrapped me in a blanket and ran to the hospital. Every time I heard this and heard the ladies sigh, I thought it was wonderful the way she saved me.

When I was two and baby Joe a few months old, Mama went to a sanatorium for tuberculosis. Daddy forgot his fears and took me to live with his mother in Phoenix. Aunt Grace cared for Joe. I remember just a little about that time: my Grandma's love, my Daddy's concern. My aunts, Florence and Martha thought I was a doll that could move and talk.

After a long time, my aunts took me to visit Mama. She seemed to be a stranger. I think she thought the same of me. When it was time to leave, I had to go potty and couldn't make my pee pee come. My exasperated aunts said hurry up, we need to go. I said not yet I need to do pee pee. It was not a happy visit. This is my own memory.

When Mama was well we lived as a family on Seventh Street, not far from Five Corners and two blocks from Ninth where my aunts and grandmother lived. I could walk to see them and they would walk to meet me. I liked to play in the kitchen to watch Mama make jam and applesauce. She would slowly peel an apple in one long unbroken spiral, trying to amuse me.

There was the day I decided to like buttermilk. I put the bottle on a chair. As I poured glass after glass it spilled out on the floor. I didn't understand why she was so angry, she had encouraged me to drink it. We tried to get acquainted. After all, we hadn't really bonded, she was away so long.

I used to lie on my back in the grass and watch the clouds. No particular thoughts, I just watched clouds.

March 2005

In The Country

When the world settles into night and day sounds fade, nocturnal creatures call to each other. Long ago in the lowering dusk my brother and I would hurry outside to wish upon a star, then play hide and seek. When dusk was far advanced Grandma called us in and lit the lamp. In the flickering light, we laughed to see our looming shadows shimmy and shake on the wall. Grandpa read Will Rogers' latest commentary from the Phoenix paper. Grandma tested our spelling and listened to our reading.

With a rhythmic rusty squeak, the windmill pumped sweet water from the deep. Water is treasured when carried even a short distance from the well. It was a great day when Uncle Jim put in pipes from pump to kitchen sink. Cold water but it was running water. For weekly baths, water was heated in an assortment of pans to fill the round washtub beside the wood burning stove. Not only was there intimacy, there was an appreciation for cleanliness.

Sheltered from the rest of the world, we learned of far away events after the fact. A bundle of papers once a week brought news, already history. The price for livestock was important.

When Grandpa drove cattle to market, five miles to the train depot, the road swarmed with bellowing steers, barking dogs and whooping cowpokes. Above it all I could hear my Grandpa's voice. Later, I begged him to tell me about the days when he was a cowboy in Texas, driving herds across the plains to Kansas.

In the country, without electricity, twilight was real. Between the day and the dark a child begins to wonder about things beyond the world, to sense a space where there is mystery. If two stars come out together, do I get two wishes?

April 2005

Blessing

They took me to see an old woman lying on a bed.
They called her Great Great Grannie.
I wondered about this.

They took me out of the warm kitchen
lit by kerosene lamps into the cold crisp night
there were stars.

The screen door squeaked as we walked into a dark house
and up some stairs to what seemed like an attic room
dark, except for a small lamp. A halo hovered
over the bed as the old woman moved her head.

Grannie, here is Patty. She stretched out a bony hand
and felt my head, running her fingers through my hair.
Winnie's child, she said. *Yes, they've come for a visit.*
I wondered about this.

My cousins took my hand and we went
back down the stairs to the warm kitchen
where we played a game of button, button
whose got the button?

I'm getting old. Will I too become some sort of
iconic figure who needs to bless
each member of a new generation.

January 2008

One Night When I Was Five

I woke up in my warm bed
but I was shivering. I pulled
up the covers, up to my ears,
then over my head.
I climbed out of bed
and walked into the night.

My flannel gown dragged
on the path and pebbles hurt my feet.
The big moon gave a bright light
so I could see the stone house.
It's not far away. I thought, *and
Grandma's door is never locked.*

Inside, I felt smooth wood on my feet
and heard the sound of breathing.
She opened her eyes and lifted
the covers for me to climb into bed.
I snuggled next to her and fell asleep.
When I think of it now I remember

that she asked no question
she knew what I needed.
I think of that little girl that I was
and I wonder at her courage
she knew what she wanted
and didn't hesitate to seek it.

October 2006

My Tree

Between the house and the vegetable garden
in Grandma's yard there was a tree, an old tree.
The orchard and the wood pile were nearby.
From the top of the tree I could hear the windmill turn.

The tree was bigger than any tree for miles around
but then there weren't many trees in the high desert
in the rocky foothills of far away mountains.

On summer afternoons in the heart of the tree
I could sit on stumps of former branches.
I could dream, I could talk to birds.

A place to be alone and not be lonely
a place to ask questions and not need answers.
A place to belong and yet be free.

July 2007

Christmas (1930)

That December was bleak. Every breath was icy and chilled the bones; too cold to make smoky fog that was so much fun to watch. The winter solstice had passed, but Pete and Joe and I didn't think that Santa would come our way. Mary was too little to worry about the possibilities. There was a fire in the big black stove and Mama suggested some games to keep us busy while she went up to the big house; she said Grandma needed her help. I was put in charge and hoped that for once my authority would not be challenged.

On Christmas eve, Mama said we should go to bed early. I argued that I didn't think Santa would find us and that if he did there was no fireplace. She said that we kids should at least do our part by going to sleep just in case he did arrive. If we were still awake he probably wouldn't stop. As it turned out, the next morning there was a little tree that hadn't been there the night before and under the tree were presents.

Grandma and Mama (I mean Santa) had been busy. They had made a rag doll for Mary and new clothes for my baby doll. The boys had fabulous muslin kites. There were new sweaters for all of us. Later I discovered what a job the sweaters had been. Someone had given them some yarn, dull grayish brown. Grandma and Mama had unraveled older sweaters and worked the bright colors into patterns on the new sweaters. They were beautiful and very warm.

December 2007

One Night When I Was Ten Years Old

Daddy parked the car on the edge of a cliff. He set the brake and put a rock in front of the wheel. Mama got out and went with him to say goodbye as he settled in for another week of work on the new high way south of Prescott. Mary, Pete and Joe were asleep on the back seat. I sat in front and watched the brake that might slip if I shut my eyes. It was a great effort to stay awake, to hold the car back from tumbling into the canyon.

Sometimes a huge truck would rumble by shaking the road, shaking the car, shaking the brake. Once I climbed out of the car to make sure the rock was still okay. I kept saying to myself, please come soon, please come soon. I knew Daddy wanted Mama to meet some of his friends who were in the bar. Then I hoped they wouldn't spend too much time in the cabin saying goodbye.

After forever, they came out. Daddy got in the car and I held my breath as he released the brake and backed the car away from the cliff. He kissed Mama, we waved to him and drove away. After a few miles she stopped the car and wept. Then she wiped her eyes. We headed home and I fell asleep.

April 2006

Avoirdupois

I have no picture of Aunt Myrtle, a sweet woman, who talked a lot in a quiet voice and was quick to laugh. She was not a good housekeeper. Her rooms were cluttered with memorabilia and Uncle Bill's inventions, such as the row of clocks that told the time in every major city around the world. She read movie magazines and had huge scrapbooks of her favorite stars and others of notorious murders of the 30's. Visiting with her was to learn of things out there in a world beyond my imagination. The first time I met her was a disaster.

When I was six I was fascinated with words and Mama had given me a definition of avoirdupois. Aunt Myrtle and Uncle Bill came for a visit and Mama wanted everything to be just right. She fussed about the house and made lovely sandwiches to serve and strawberry shortcake. But she had not prepared me for the occasion.

When Auntie arrived, she hugged me close to her voluptuous body. I caught my breath. With the wisdom of my year I declared, *Now, Mama, I understand what you meant by avoirdupois.* Auntie dropped me and sat down.

Mama gasped and sent me out to play. *But I wanted tea with you,* I wailed as I went to my room to sulk.

March 2004

Rumble Seat

One hundred miles on a Sunday night
as startled birds, flushed from chaparral
took flight and road runners
dashed down the middle of the lane.

Grotesque shadows receded
out of sight across the sand as if
the desert had put on strange attire
for a moonlight masquerade.

I rode in the rumble seat with
Prince, a German shepherd
on the four-hour trip from Phoenix
after visiting Mom and Dad.

There were weird night noises when
we stopped from time to time
to stretch our legs and let Prince
run about. The cacti stood as sentinels.

One hundred miles, cold and lonely
I cuddled up with the big dog
who wanted warmth of my body
as much as I needed his.

February 2005

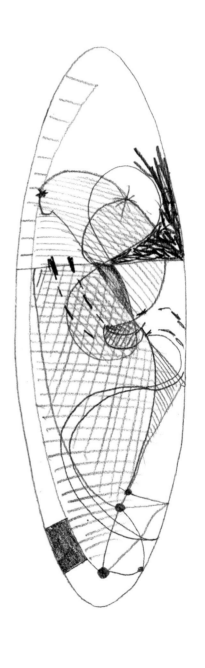

The Space Between

I was just a toddler
when Mama went away
to a sanatorium.

Months later
she tried
to please
and pamper me
as any mother
would
but I had lost
my trust in her.

She tried to curl my hair
like Shirley Temple's hair
but the ringlets
fell down
and looked like
worn out excelsior.

Through the years
each tried to reach
the other but neither
could step into
the space between.

August 2011

Chicken Soup

The recipe calls for a chicken
cut in pieces.

Auntie Maude loved chicken soup.
She would amuse me as she wandered
through the years, meandering along
by-ways as she talked, getting lost
in explanations of who was related
to whom and who wore what to where.

As I said, start with a chicken
put the pieces in a pot, add water.

My Grandma would twirl a chicken
in the air to break its neck.
Once I was attacked by a rooster
when I went to gather eggs.
She heard my screams and whacked
that rooster's head off with an ax
then made a pot of chicken soup.

As I was saying put the chicken in the pot
add onions, celery, carrots, rosemary and bay.

Mama believed in spices.
Even when the cupboard and the frig
seemed bare, she could create
a gourmet meal and decorate each dish
with parsley, carrot curls or radish roses.

Did I say the chicken needs to simmer 'til it's
falling off the bones? Serve with a dry white wine.

Remember what a fuss Julia Child
would make about which wine to serve with what
and she would sample as she cooked.
I'll swear she seemed a little tight
by the time the show was over.

Would you like some Chardonnay
or would you prefer Merlot?

October 2004

A Two Mile Walk
Along a Cliff of Years

Roses and marguerites peak over a garden fence and turn their faces to the sun. Way out in the water, two fishermen are in a boat. A little rip tide follows one wave and bumps into the next, while a lone sandpiper hurries back and forth to peck the sand; another simply watches as the surf breaks on the beach.

> My brother Joe caught a thirty pound bass in the surf north of Pedro Point before he went to fight and die in France. Beach houses were windswept behind hedges of marguerites. I was a little girl filling a box with driftwood and dragging it up the hill.

Doves cling to the cliff and watch the water. A couple sits on a bench put there in memory of a surfer who drowned off this rocky shore. It's starting to rain, I need to hurry home and build a fire against the cold.

> Joe and I took turns blowing our breaths to fan the flames, a game of being first to get the log to light. We sat and read poems to each other. He had a book and I had one, we raced to keep the rhythm going, funny and sad, laughter and silence. I went away to college; he went away to war.

There's a *For Sale* sign on a house with pink roses on the fence. Years ago, our house on the hill was sold. I don't know who lives there now. I have driven by and paused to look at the red cement steps leading up to the door of the house with the marguerites.

> I see myself as a little girl dragging driftwood up the hill. My brother is coming to help me carry the box up the long, steep, red steps.

Drops of rain have disappeared; doves still cling to the cliff.

November 2003

Algebra

For two days I was passionately
in love with the boy who sat
across the aisle from me in algebra.
His hair was blond
and he combed it neatly back
but it always escaped
to fall onto his tanned forehead.
I remember that his eyes were blue.

On the third day,
soon after class began
the object of my affections
extended his leg into the aisle.
His freshly washed jeans
were just like the ones
worn by my brother, Pete.

Suddenly, I remembered
when years before
Pete had torn the head from one
of my paper dolls. After waving
it in the air while I screamed
he threw it in the fire.

I had designed more than
a hundred lovely gowns
for her. I tried and tried to draw
another head but finally I threw
the elegant wardrobe into the fire
along with the headless doll.

This incident colored my opinion
of boys. I realized this boy
was a boy like any other.
I fell out of love.
He never knew the part
he played in my emotions.
I didn't realize
my equation didn't balance.

June 2011

A Learning Curve

In 1944, I learned that I liked pepper on my steak. And fried potatoes. That year I tried to learn to cook the food my husband remembered that his mother cooked. I learned how long I could read a book or magazine and still have dinner on the table. I learned to listen to the scuttlebutt and buy a ticket on the train before everyone else knew the boys were moving out. I learned how to find a room to rent in a town crowded with soldiers and soldiers' wives. And then, I learned to say, *Goodbye*.

August 2005

Values Change

Every time I put a coffee can in the recycling I think of Nina, my husband's mother. It was 1945 and I lived with her while Les was overseas. She had a large collection of coffee cans in her garage. They were a scarce item in those days when all available metal was going for the war effort. The tight pre-war cans were wonderful for storage. She was reluctant to give up any of them. They were perfect for sending cookies to the Philippines and later to Okinawa. Once in a while, she would offer me one of her hoard; then gracious *thank you's* and *you're welcomes* would be exchanged; but I never felt I could cross a line to ask her for a coffee can. It's strange; her son would be receiving the gift. Maybe a tad of jealousy? I wondered then; I wonder now, every time I throw away a coffee can. Of course it goes into the recycling but I am tempted to put it on a shelf in the garage. It would once have been a precious object, equal to its weight in gold.

August 2010

Pushing Carriages

Two women are pushing
their babies in carriages
on the path along the cliff.
I mean this as reality
and metaphor. The sun
has not yet climbed to noon
I mean this as before.

Soon troubles of the world
will be pounding at the door.
Do not let them in as they
will drain the bank account
and blood account and heart
and soul. This I know
and give fair warning
which no one will heed.
I mean this as before.

April, 2008

My mother was washing my back, *You have a very nice back.* She didn't hint at the loads the little back would carry, the wars, the wondering, the worrying, the births, the caring. The waiting

for the proverbial straw.

June, 2005

Two Turtles

I

I was a little girl wading in the creek
on a hot summer day, feeling sand
between my toes. I dumped cold water
on hot rocks, and laughed to see
steam gather and fade. I played
a game of jumping the stream, back
and forth. In wide places I bounced
across on rocks. Suddenly, a rock moved.

I screamed. Dad woke up from a nap.
The boys quit digging a pool for minnows.
Mom stopped watching the clouds.
We took the turtle home, and put him in a pen.
For hours I sat nearby, talking and watching.
He didn't return my attention like a kitten
or a chicken or a lamb. He just sat inside his shell.
I kept talking, knowing he heard my voice.

The boys taunted me, *If he bites your finger*
he won't let go 'till it thunders. I studied
the sky. Only one tiny cloud near the horizon.
I defended my position near the turtle
examining the patterns of his shell
that copied the color of rock. I told
the boys to stay away, *It's my turtle!*
I'm the one who stepped on him.

I watched and waited and patiently waited.
Finally his calloused head came out, inquiring eyes looked over
the situation.
The next morning I found the pen
overturned, the turtle was gone.
I searched the creek all summer.
Loss and longing, wonder and worry
I just don't know about turtles.

II

Many years later, near the coast
going home from a picnic, I suddenly
stopped the car. We thought we saw
a rock in the middle of the road.
It's a turtle! Can we keep him, Mom?
No, you just don't know about turtles.
My son held his ground, we couldn't go on.
Inquiring eyes came out of the shell.

The kids all shouted, *Let's keep him*
Mom. Please, Mom, please.
We took him home, and put
him in a pen. All day I watched
the boy watch the turtle. That night
about eleven, I heard a door.
I'm just checking on the turtle, Mom.
In the morning the turtle was gone.

The taunting began, *There are people*
in this town who make soup out of turtles.
He went back to the mountain, I know he did.
What about the cars out on the highway?
Early in the morning there aren't very many.
We searched for days and never a sign.
I told him that turtles go their own way.
You just don't know about turtles.

Althea, Nina and Maude

Three women sit on a bench.
The photographer says, *Smile*
now hold it. Right there.
Say, Cheese! Just a minute.
I need to focus again.
Their chins tilt up expectantly
their half smiles wait patiently
for this moment to be recorded.

All dressed up with somewhere
to go. Their make-up has been
carefully applied, their hats
have turned up brims.
Wherever they are going
they know they are ready.

Althea and Nina are cousins
friends since childhood. What
explains the presence of Maude?
Only funerals or weddings bring
Althea and Maude together.
As for Nina and Maude, her
sister-in-law, there has always been
rivalry between them and some
slight tension when they are together.

Flowers bloom beside the door.
Maude is wearing white gloves.
There are no wraps laying
on the bench. It must be late summer.
Perhaps they have met for lunch.

I think of their toughness, their instinct
for survival, for caring, for family.
A fireplace in the background, the wall
and the bench are all of well-worn brick.
Althea, Nina and Maude, gracious
with each other, they have learned
to weather the storms, to let go
of bitterness. They dress with care
when invited to lunch and smile
patiently for the photographer.

October 1993

we smiled

pictures of places
now forgotten
important when
the shutter clicked

mountains somewhere
more mountains
more trees

rocks, seagulls, fish
more fish
i remember this lake
this smiling couple
who is this child

pictures at a reunion
cousins meeting cousins
burying old feuds
some still smoldering
some causing small explosions

pictures with no names
names with no faces
time takes time away
only yesterday
the shutter clicked
we smiled

May 2006

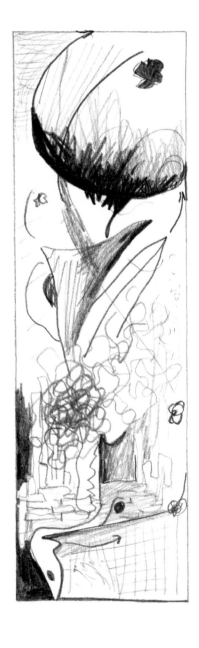

Fashion

I've seen a lot of fashion
skirts going up and down
and almost disappearing.
When a blouse shows
lower than the jacket
I remember my grandma
saying to my brothers
I'll sew lace
all around your shirt tails
if you don't tuck them in.

December 2007

Lately

Lately I've noticed people walking away
before they hear the punch line of my story
the story they hadn't heard before
because we had never met before.
Stranger to me, still stranger.

The clerk was friendly when she took my money
telling me, sweetly, to have a nice day.
I began to share my plans, she turned
to another customer without another word.
This is all just anecdotal, doesn't prove a thing.

This peaceful room is charming.
My books, my crystal and my china
family pictures on the walls
the floor is not cluttered with games or toys.
The TV is on to fill the room with voices.

October 2007

Creamed Tuna

My mother-in-law's recipe was simple
white sauce made with creamery butter
and a bit of flour to thicken fresh whole milk
add tuna and serve over white bread toast.
This was always lunch for company.

A bride tries to satisfy a hubby's appetite
for his mama's cooking, so I perfected
tuna on toast. Once I added onion juice
and one time, lemon zest. Boldly I sautéed
onion, bell pepper and a bit of parsley.
It was an easy jump from there to potato
casserole. A few years later the kids
liked creamed tuna with potato chips.

Now alone and wanting comfort food
I open a can of mushroom soup and heat it
in the microwave while I find the whole wheat
bread. Memory brings a picture of everyone
at the table waiting for the toast.

October 2008

Fulfillment of Desire

I played piano on my Grandma's porch striking the bench in a slow romantic rhythm, then sliding into a wild and frantic dance. Emotion traveled through my fingers across imaginary black and white ivories. I wanted to play a real piano, to really, really play.

Then I was tap dancing on the lawn, my bare feet beating a tattoo on the grass as I did traveling steps all around the house. I heard the applause and bowed to the make-believe audience.

Mama said we were going to move. *I just made friends at this school — and I'm halfway through the book about the winning of the west. When we move they'll be studying something new. I'll be behind the other kids. Why, Mama, do we have to move again?*

At the new school, Sister said I could be in the choir. She put me in the front row so I wouldn't influence the other kids to sing off key. One day in the auditorium I stood on the stage, stumbling over a poem I had memorized. Something about *foolish questions.* Something very cute. I was petrified. All I could do was taste the words that were caught in my throat.

Funny you should ask how desires have been fulfilled. It's not a foolish question. I have had successes in my life, it's true, but it amuses and amazes me that my children and my children's children are doing all the things I used to want to do — and doing so much more.

March 2004

Sixty Years

I wuld like to write a poem
about Mary Dolores Hernan
and Robert Harvey Mullis.
Poetry does not suffice.
Their life requires a novel
or a series, a saga of life,
partly mystery, partly romance.
A true history of recent times.

Include a recipe for life,
a few spoonfuls of sugar,
a dash of salt, some pepper.
Add herbs and spices to taste.
Stir in some children,
commitment and caring.
Top off with neighbors and friends.
Blend all together with love.

Take all the above and add
an enormous *How To* manual.
Even these all together
are not enough to describe
the years of living, of love,
and commitment in which
        Mary and Bob
                have become true artists.

November 2008

Michael and Denise
on their 25th Wedding Anniversary

To Michael and Denise, my thoughts now fly
Like rain that seeks a welcome in the ground.
Love's secrets, you have solved and now know why
No greater joy than marriage can be found
Or to be parents feathering your nest
For three handsome sons and a darling girl.
You taught them well, to look for what is best
To give us all, the love that is a pearl.
We toast the two of you, a happy pair
A wonder in these days. We celebrate!
Lift up your glass and sing and then declare
Life is good, friends are true. Commemorate
This day with new resolve, with wine, with food
With sons and daughter, friends, for all is good.

September 2010

For Jason

Your great, great grandfather* said, *Take care of your pennies and the dollars will take care of themselves.*

Your great, great grandmother* loved the soil and her vegetable garden fed all of us. People came from miles around to see her beautiful flower garden. They wondered why she would spend so much effort on flowers when it was such a struggle to make a living.

Your great grandfather* told me he always looked for good in everyone he met.

These are words from people you will never know but their blood is in you. They were survivors and passed their strength to you.

If you —
  Live your life fully from edge to edge
  and always be true to yourself
  you will find the golden fleece.

* Julius Sylvanus Reagan
Dora Alice Wilkerson Reagan
John Joseph Hernan Jr.

May 2002

Topsy-turvy Days

Once there were topsy-turvy days
of diapers hanging in the sun
a time of neighbors gossiping
across the lines of wind blown clothes
hours pushing strollers in the park
slides and swings and up in the air
and down and here we go again
up and over the world so wide.

At dinner someone spills the milk.
Then as evening disappears, there are
dancers in soft footed sleepers, some
with bare feet in flannel gowns
over and over and one more time.
goodnight moon and songs repeated

God bless each one of us by name
and all creatures of land, sea and air.

Each day's work was never done
I thought the world would wait.
And yet the years relentlessly
were rushing through the century.
Each time is best and so is now
but still it seems there was a time
I didn't know was magical
or that those days were full of grace.

April 2005

I Know His Smile

for Alexander Michael Grube

I have a new grandson
born from moon glow
and tall mountains.
Gazelles and elephants
lions and deer know him.
They gave him grace
strength, courage and perception.
His heart is pure
as water that flows
from a spring at the center
of a mountain.
Though I haven't seen him
I have seen his smile.

November 2003

Walking Along The Cliff

Where the path curves there is
a stone wall where swallows have
built their nests in holes carved
by the water. All day they dart

in and out of the rocks. Sometimes
late at night, cars come screeching
around the curve and go over the edge
right over the homes of the swallows.

Here is a stone bridge reaching into
the bay where the waves are strong.
Mama painted a picture of it when
it was longer and there was another arch.

There is Dee's house. Once I gathered
poppy seeds in her garden. I want to stop
and say hello. Then I remember
she is not there to open the door.

A thin strip of gold and silver lights
are beginning to glow along the horizon.
The clouds are lifting.
A lone seagull calls across the waves.

October 2004

At The Beach

The waves rush up the beach
she screams and then will run.
She dances and she laughs
when has there been such fun?

She knows that the water
touches the shore somewhere
beyond the curve of earth
but now she does not care.

* * *

In years to come they'll say
that it was for the best.
Her life was long and she
deserved a well earned rest.

They'll watch a little boat
far out beyond the waves.
Their thoughts will wander off
to loved ones in their graves.

This is what she wanted.
She told us her desire
for tide to claim her ash
when taken from the fire.

To drift around the world
whatever the will of the sea
to places far and strange
wherever they may be.

May 2003

Peter James Hernan, Commander, USN
June 5, 1927 – November 29, 2004

Salmon swim up the creek
to spawn and die.
Peter's ashes were scattered there.
Irish songs were meant to cheer.
The gun salute to honor.
The bugler stood in the cold wet field
and taps echoed through the trees
and across the hills to Mt. Rainier.

He went to sleep in his favorite chair
while watching morning news
in the room where his medals
and citations were all there
on the walls with cartoons
and comic commendations.

Hanging there was the sword
that was with the empty boots
on the riderless horse
at Admiral Halsey's funeral procession.
Daddy gave Peter the sword
at his first commission.
Years later when the Admiral's sword
could not be found they borrowed his.

Salmon swim up the creek
Peter's ashes were scattered there
with the grief of sons
and daughters, their children
and their children's children.
His mourning wife
his friends
his sisters' sadness
mingled with the mist.

High tide will come at sunset
and wash all out to the seas
he commanded during war.
Out through Liberty Bay
where sea gulls fly and wild geese
set down to rest. The birds
he fed each day will look for him
and find that he has sailed away.

January 2005

Stars

As a child, in the mountains of Arizona, I watched each evening to see the first star and make a wish. On summer nights I count stars, I cannot see them all and cannot count the ones I see. Why do some stars fall out of the sky?

In Zambia, in the flat middle of the continent of Africa, the sky is wide, the stars are bright. One night, inside a club in Ndola, the music played, the dancers danced, drinks were poured and hors d'oeuvres passed. I heard a crash of broken glass but no one had dropped a tray. I went outside to catch my breath. There in the garden I looked at the stars and wondered what is beyond the beyond.

Many miles north on the other side of the Congo, in the Central African Republic, on a road stretching into the jungle, a military vehicle struck and killed my very dear friend. That night, for the first time, low on the horizon, I saw the Southern Cross.

October 2003

memorial

we live with death
and die with life
leaving behind cold ashes
perhaps a spark
perhaps a flame
sometimes a roaring fire

March 2006

My Mentor

If you had been my neighbor
when I was ten years old
I would have looked to you
as to an older sister. I would
have watched you curl your hair
with a hot curling rod.
I would have driven Mama crazy
with tales of your exploits.

Fern has a beaux, Mama.
She curled her hair and put
something icky on her face.
Why is she so silly just because
she's going to a dance
and he'll be there?

At twenty you would have
put up with my hero worship
told me I would grow up
soon enough. You would have
listened to my woes, given me
advice about a freckled kid
I kind of had a crush on.

You would have read me poems
and told me about Amy Lowell's
lost lover. It's now, not then and
I am sitting at your feet admiring
how you live your life, how you
support my stumbling steps.

*Written in memory of Fern Tobey, who
inspired us in the Chaparral poetry workshop.*

March 2005

What Can I Say

Age does not bring wisdom
it brings aching bones
and sagging breasts
and in the night a reaching
out to find an empty space.

Today a sudden sadness
of a neighbor gone; my quick
remorse, remembering how
I snubbed her when she
seemed to interrupt my day.

Age brings letters with details
of disease, of disappointments,
hips that need replacing
broken bones, new knees
moving from a family home.

Earth was born by an explosion
from the sun, ejected in anger
or orgasmic passion. Some stars
will fall but I can't care about
the whims of the universe.

I skipped to the Universe because
I don't know how to answer
letters that come in the mail
full of trials and tribulations.
I don't know what to say.

Singed

Beauty of moth
      flying to light
perfume of wings
      touching fire.
Now no more soaring to heights
      but trying
fluttering
      only fluttering
         courage of moth.

Clare would say
      Tell me about the color of the wings
let me feel the softness of feathers
compare the moth with — whatever.
But this is about the
      essence of moth.
This is about survival
      and struggle
         the need to fly.

April 2006

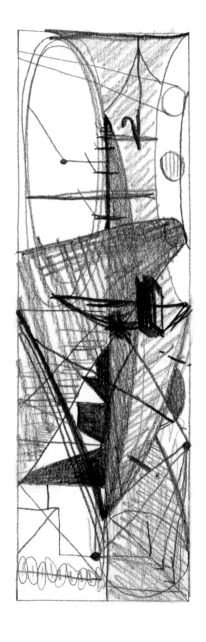

Diagnosis

When I put my pants on backwards
I wonder if it's Alzheimers
I realize that if I wonder
then it can't be, so I take them off
and put them on again.
My shirt has a label in the back
I know that's right.

May 2007

Keeping Alive

She puts clippings
of leggy marguerites in water
with ivy and a rose.

I pulled a weed
she took it and put it
in the crowded jar.
Mary, that's a weed

She replied *the water
will keep it alive.*
She wants them all to live
and tries to save the ones
that cling to life.

We tell each other
stories of the past.
Hers keep changing.

Once she told me that
Aunt Grace died in her sleep.
The week before she said
she held her aunt's hand
all day so the angels
couldn't carry her away.

She dreams of little cabins
by the water and says
she wants to live there.

It's cool and quiet
under trees and fishermen
are mending their nets.

I don't tell her that
this place does not exist.
Perhaps it's in her heaven.

September 2007

The Crown

We used to talk
about our days
our children
husbands, houses
and our recipes.

We used to joke
that in heaven
we would wear crowns
adorned with jewels
earned by deeds
of dedication.

That idea was tucked away
with all lost memories.
We slowly learned
it really added up to love.

Each day brought a joy
perhaps a struggle
sometimes grief
or thankfully a friend.
Sometimes
just survival.

Then, there came
a long slow pilgrimage
before the mystery
would be revealed.

Mary never realized
how many jewels
she earned, and now
the overwhelming
brilliance of her crown
shines with the stars.

May 2011

The Dark Forest

I met an old woman who hurried along
saying, *Where are the children?*
They should be sleeping. I must find
the children and put them to bed.
I patted her hand
      Yes, yes, my dear
      Yes, yes, my dear

Then as I walked I met another
who tugged at my elbow, *I've counted the silver*
something is missing. I folded the sheets
and I must count the silver. I must fold the sheets.
I patted her hand
      Yes, yes, my dear
      Yes, yes, my dear

The hall was wide where a woman was walking
she looked in my eyes with despair.
He hasn't come back. He went into the forest.
Wringing her hands and sighing and saying
His dinner is waiting. He hasn't come back.
I patted her hand
      Yes, yes, my dear
      Yes, yes, my dear

The hall was long in the dark woods
where I walked to visit my husband.
I peeked in each door and finally
found him listening to a woman
who was singing an aria in a sweet voice
no words just clear full tones.
I patted her hand
>   *Yes, yes, my dear*
>   *Yes, yes, my dear*

Their souls met at some incomprehensible level
as he looked at her in adoration,
he clapped his hands, she bowed her head.
I kissed him then.
>   *Yes, yes, my dear*
>   *Yes, yes, my dears*

September 2003

He Danced

He danced along the cliff
and greeted strangers.
They saw his joy
and knew that life was good.

His social graces kept him safe
in a dark place.
He had an inner light.

September 2004

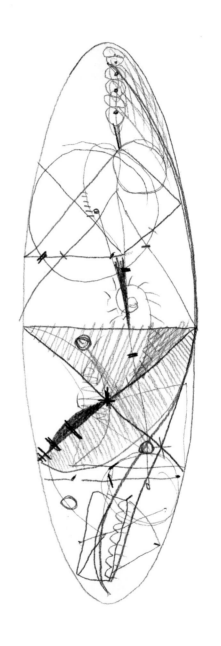

Big Dipper
Zambia

If I look at the moon tonight, I know
that in twelve hours at home
they'll be seeing the same moon.
When I look at the stars
they're not the same stars.
I thought they would be the same.
We're in the Southern Hemisphere.
We're on the other side of the world.
At night I see the Southern Cross.
I wish I knew something about the stars.
The Big Dipper is all I've ever really
been sure of; finding it is like
finding an old friend. There it is, low
on the horizon but it's upside down.
Here on the other side of the world
everything is different. Nothing is the same
and the Big Dipper is upside down.

September 2011

Animal Stories

Zambia, Africa, 1971

#1
In Lusaka
the boys found geckos
on their walls in our hotel.
A lady from India said
to leave them alone
*they'll clean the room of all
the little biting creatures.*

#2
We had a house
in Ndola with a garden.
Chameleons
kept changing colors
as they climbed
brown branches
to hide in green leaves.

#3
The children left crumbs of cake
scattered here and there.
Too tired, I went to bed.
In the night grease ants
came in and cleaned the floor.

#4
In their separate kai in the backyard
David and Patrick had a monkey.
When he wouldn't be housebroken
even they became disgusted
and grudgingly gave him up.

#5
Donald found a cocoon
on a dry branch
and put it on the bookcase.
In the morning hundreds
of praying mantis spread
across the school books
the novels and the family bible.

Bearing Witness

It's said once long ago
a Spanish galleon was wrecked
on Galway Bay. One of my ancestors
escaped the English there.
I remembered the story
as I watched the waves.

The Wall in China wanders
like a snake across the miles
across the mountains.
Once long ago hand-hewn stones
were put there by peasants
conscripted to build defenses.
I have a photo of the rugged walk.

Standing in the sun
looking for some shade
I found a tree where
slaves were sold once
long ago in Zambia.
I felt that I had been
there in the past.

In desert air, in wilderness
I sat on a rock in the hills where
long ago the Baptist roamed.
I found his spirit there.

According to St. Helena
who claimed she found
the true cross, we walked
the streets where
Jesus walked, once
long ago in Jerusalem.

February 2011

Ndola, Zambia, 1971

The doctor at the hospital today was Chinese. He didn't give us herbs, just ointment for the sore on Chris's leg. With winter and summer all backwards, he said it would take a while for him to build up a resistance. The out-patient clinic was crowded. We had been waiting a long time in a long line, then we all sat with the doctor in the same big room. We watched each examination and heard each diagnosis. The doctor, the Chinese doctor was so kind. He was talking to a man who was holding a very sick little boy, maybe three years old. A woman was translating what the doctor said into Cibemba. He told the man that his child had TB. The man nodded, then he just looked at his boy. His expression was so ... resigned. The doctor wanted to put the child in the hospital. The man nodded to show he understood and then he just looked at his boy some more. Many of the mothers with their toddlers, also had a baby on their backs. They were all quiet, wondering, I think, about their own children. I know how I felt. We all felt the same. All of us felt the same, for the child, for the man, for our own children.

This is a found prose poem, taken from my play, "Nshima." At this time the USA had no relations with China. They had removed all aid when Zambia accepted China's offer to build a railroad from the port in Mozambique. The USA and Britain had refused to do this.

August 2007

An Oyster

An oyster shell is rough
the inside polished
to protect the living flesh
perhaps a pearl.

The world is crusty and complex
sometimes burdensome
oppressive. In places
millions crowd into cruel cities.
Many pearls are there.

October 2000

In China

I fill my fanny pack
with camera, film
and lipstick, strap it
'round my waist
in front of me.

I am pregnant again
not with child
but with pictures
of
      the
               Orient.

October 2000

The Three Gorges Dam

Mist rises from the Yangtze
over the ancestral home.
Bones of my father
must be moved to another place
and laid in soil he never tilled.
The Yangtze will rise
silt will cover our fields
the trees will drown in the red water.

The population of China is one billion, two hundred million people.
The Three Gorges Dam means the displacement of one and a third million people.

Written while traveling on the river in Elizabeth II. Yichang is known as "Gateway
of the Three Gorges" and is where we embarked to visit the sight of the new dam.

October 2000

Too foggy for pictures

The banks of the Yangzte
emerge from the morning mist.
There are low hills and plots
divided by hedge rows and trees.

I see farmsteads behind levees
built to keep the water in its place.
Here and there the banks are covered
with rock or cement blocks.

Each year the river cuts through
the barricades and takes
its toll in lives and land.
Loaded barges travel to Shanghai.

Water buffalo graze unperturbed
by the flood that will come
to drop alluvial mud
when levees break, to be built again.

The energy of the river
is overpowering.
My journey is peaceful
the river is not.

Crops flourish, millions eat.
The river gives and takes away.
That is the power, the danger
and the bounty of the Yangzte.

October 2000

I Saw the Gorges from a Tour Boat

Broken cliffs plunge ten thousand feet,
their wall-like faces ragged in mist ...
There the curve-bound pools spin nine times round,
swelling and subsiding, and the fierce currents
roar like thunder, dart with lightning speed.
–Kuo Pu, 3rd Century

In nineteen-nineteen, Sun Yat Sen proposed
a plan to tame the temperamental Yangtze
to tap the power of the river
to reduce pollution from coal burning plants.

November, two thousand two.
A sound bite, a photo flash, officials in business suits
push rocks into the Yangtze to symbolize a new phase
of construction of the biggest dam in the world.
Meter by meter, the river begins to rise.

A million people and more
live in old cities and villages that will disappear.

By June, two thousand three,
Zhangfei Temple will be submerged, then brick by brick
rebuilt on higher ground to commemorate
an ancient battle. Water will continue to slowly rise.

Two thousand nine.
Peaks of mountain ranges become islands
in a lake extending to Chongquing.
Sea going vessels will carry produce from the provinces
across the new great water to Shanghai.

From before history there have been floods along the river.

In the thirties, in the city of Wuhan,
for ninety days, people were held captive
by the water. For many hundred miles around
farmlands were inundated. Livestock lost.
Diseases followed. Thousands died.
The world wept. Lindy flew to China
to survey damages and help in the rescue.

Levees built but always floods.
In nineteen-ninety eight, thousands drowned
as water filled the narrow streets of Jinjang.
In the fields, one tenth of China's grain was lost.

Levees broken, built again.

Three Gorges Dam is a battlefield in a war with nature.
There are concerns
about climate changes
and removing silt that will flow into the reservoir.
Consider the Yangtze dolphin
what will become of the Chinese sturgeon?

Explosives have just destroyed Fengjie
it's streets where poets walked.
Mud and red water of the Yangtze
slowly cover the old towns.
Baidi City and Shibao are submerged.
Water is rising in the ancient river port of Wanxian.

Time and money are running out as water
fills the gorges, Xiling, Wu Xia and Qutang.
Treasures are moved to higher ground
as Archeologists scurry to discover artifacts.

I saw the gorges from a tour boat
the mountains actually look Chinese.

I saw numbers that mark the level the river will reach.
I saw towns beginning to grow near mountaintops
new apartments have toilets and running water.
I saw stone steps on the face of a cliff
steps carved by an ancestor
to reach his, now doomed, fields.

I didn't see farmers who grieve for lost crops.
I didn't hear women saying goodbye as families scatter
from old neighborhoods to live in new towns.

Where are the friends we knew?
Where is the pancake vendor?
What will we do for breakfast?

December 2002

The Great Wall

I stand on the wall
the steps are steep
the surface rough.
An old lady with no banister to grasp
I try to keep my balance
as the crowd moves around me.

I stand on the wall
as my thoughts drift
through the centuries like a lost soul
wandering through the hills.
Ancient rulers built the wall
walled cities were the fashion then.
Why not a wall across the width of China?
They did not count the human cost.

I stand on the wall
and look at the massive stones
put in place by peasants drafted
from the villages. Their sweat
their blood mingled in the mortar.
I watch the faces of Chinese tourists
from the provinces, who are inspired
by the unbelievable achievement.

I stand on the wall
and watch how it meanders
into the far mountains
like a giant snake.
The Chinese say it is like a dragon.
The people are patient and strong
enduring like the wall.

October 2000

Found Poetry: Acrobats and a Magic Act

I am in the bar of a steamer on the Yangtze
sipping a bourbon on rocks
writing statistics in my journal.

I jot down some notes.

At a nearby table two couples, share views
on tours and life, remembering
when they were young in London.

The river flows on.

One woman with gray corkscrew curls
recounts her story. *Five girls came out of a box
that only had room for one.*

Of course it's an illusion.

Her companion smiles as the others nod.
*Every now and then George
gave me a poke in the ribs.*

I do doze off you know.

The wine has been too much.
Oh, yes, I don't drink at all at home.
Rum — I do like a drop of rum.

It was during the war I got introduced to rum.

A couple of us girls went out together.
The fellows were twenty-five, I guess.
We were only sixteen. It was alright

you know, for the soldiers.

If you stop in Shanghai
be sure to see the show
acrobats and a magic act.

October 2000

Lobby of the Taiwan Hotel, Beijing

Busy people talk of trips
   talk of children
   talk of troubles
   talk of death

Busy people hurry to the wall
   to the temples
   to the shops
   to the tombs

Busy tourists hurry as I watch
   and wonder as I wait
   where are they going
   what are they fearing
      talking all the way

October 2000

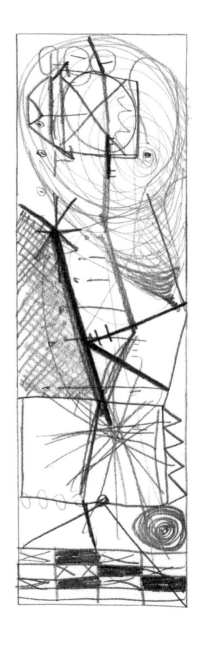

Remnants

I try to hold on
to the boney fingers of the past.
The breath is un-even
the heart beat slows.
Where does a dream go?

I know I'm getting old
because I'm getting grouchy
because things are moving too fast
because my children
can manage their own affairs.

The world goes round
without a sound
all the tension
all the strife
is on the surface
filled with life
loving, dying

mountains crumble
birds are singing
birds are flying
earthquakes rumble.

May 2010

The Woman In The Mirror

The twinkle in her eye
reminds me of my mother
the wrinkles on her cheek
I can't remember who.
She needs a bit of rouge.

I've met her someplace, sometime
before her hair turned gray.
If we meet I wonder
would I like her?
I know we have a lot to share.

March 2007

poetry reading

the poet was small
i mean small in stature
but strong and
meaningful in voice
a full voice
full of meaning
a clear voice
her meaning was clear
her images vivid
surrounding sorrow
encapsulating it
in metaphor
where she had courage
to fight a dragon
courage to look it
straight in the eye
and see it slink away
she was young
but not too young to know
the dragon would
be back another day

November 2003

Through a Dark Valley

Melancholy overcomes me on this
damp, depressing day. Regrets
and bitterness pull me toward
a cesspool of anger and resentment.
What is this place where

I have pushed my demons
where the murky air is filled
with lamentations of remorse?
I see no way to transform it
to claim it as a necessary passage
through a dark valley.

Suddenly — the sun appears
just as the day is ending.
As I watch it slips into the sea.
Long strips of gold cut through
the clouds and pierce my soul.

November 2003

In The Shower

First I soap my right underarm
then beneath my breast
across my chest
to my other arm
my tummy and so forth.

When I rinse, the pattern
is different, first
the back of my neck
with the shower massage
then my spine and so forth.

The point being, why
am I set in this illogical
process. There I am morning
after morning – first
the right underarm and so forth.

I'm too young to be set in my ways.
That would be a sign of senility.
So I'm keeping watch on my
comings and goings. I might find
something important and so forth.

October 2005

Sorority

Judy, Rae, Nancy, Jean, Marie
and Dotty. Anne, Beth, Deb
and Faye. Gayle, Julia, Noreen
and Charlotte. Betty, Caroline
and Sue. I've joined a sorority
I didn't want to join.

I was nominated for membership
by a mammogram. I tried
to avoid the election
but was chosen anyway.
I tried to resign and finally was
resigned to what I had to do.

With a purple pen, he was marking
on my breast, my left breast.
Will it be a pretty picture? I asked.
Do you want a happy face?
In the mirror, when I looked
there was a circle with a smile.

The initiation rites were quite severe
wrought with anxiety, some might say
pain. In case you want to know
there was surgery and consultation
with oncologists. Photos, x-rays
sonograms, cat-scans and the tattoo
with the purple pen, all to give
direction to the linear accelerator
that was created years after Marie Curie.

Sitting with sisters
We share stories, as we wait
for the daily absolution.
Lying on a narrow bench
I put my trust in the great robot
that sends a spirit
into my breast to destroy
remnants of the enemy.

April 2005

one of life's problems

a triangle of silk
or long rectangle
to wrap casually
about the throat
to knot or not to knot
let fly or tie
sedately at the neck
perhaps a turban
on a bad hair day

soft silk tossed
across my shoulders
feels seductive
truth be told, I have
no way with a scarf
although I am intrigued
with possibilities

the designs delight me
I try, I tie, I furl, tuck in, let fly
I play the matador
and laugh then carefully
I fold it neatly and put
it in the drawer

January 2007

Mirror, Mirror on the Wall

We do Qigong in a room
with a mirrored wall.
My eyes stray
from cloud hands
to see the reflection
of a stranger, a mimic
of my every move.

With each motion
I hear an echo, rhythmic
and demanding, who
are you? breathe in
who are you? breathe out.
The quest never ends.

September 2009

Cold Feet

I am lying awake, wishing
there were someone to warm my feet
wishing for a warm back to cuddle up to.
I'll fill a bottle with hot water
and bring it back to bed.
Then I'll try to think of something
other than cold feet.

Poems about old age are not as popular
as poems of youth. Poems of dying
are also well received.
Why this skip to my loo, my darling
between young and dead?

Tragedy is daring
old age is dreary.
Young love sings to the stars.
Love in old age is
oh, my god, not them.

Youth looks at a waterfall
and finds fantastic metaphors.
Old age sits by a waterfall.

> *Friend, we just keep going. and yet —*
> *la, dee, da, da, da — something about life —*
> *shining through the water — which flows over rocks—*
> *over whatever — and eventually reaches the sea.*

Just as my life does.

> *Old friend, I have sat here many times —*
> *You and I are both survivors.*
> *You've pushed a few rocks off the cliff*
> *but your channel remains the same.*
> *When you were diverted, you broke through*
> *and confounded those who would confine you.*

My feet are getting warm, lulled by the memory
of your melody, I'm drifting off to sleep.

November 2003

Poem on Poem

Stone on stone
some poems are built
some are cloud on cloud.
Some are built of logs
with wooden pegs.

Some poems have doors
to small secluded nooks.
Some have long halls
that lead to grand salons.
Some open windows
to fresh vistas of the world.

A poet can ride on clouds
and look for stars. Fly high
above the hills to see
the other side. But then
my muse begins to scream
Come down you're far to high
you're much too old to fly.

November 2007

Find Meaning Where You Can

Life is a tragedy to be lived.
He said. She laughed.
I say a comedy. What could
be funnier than you and me?

Love on either side and in between
the gifts of truth, of beauty.
All are one, the poet said.

So they agreed.
We have gained everything
in tears and laughter.

My Head Is Turning To A Sieve

My head is turning to a sieve, it may be brass, aluminum or pewter. My choice is granite-ware like Grandma's baking pans that were covered with light and dark gray spots. If I stood on a box near the big black stove where she cooked, I could watch her work. She told me her secrets: knead the bread for fifteen minutes, don't turn pancakes until all the bubbles have burst, sauté onions before you add them to the stew. Getting back to the sieve full of holes my thoughts are as scattered as if I threw them out into the desert, the high desert, where Grandpa's cattle grazed. We would go there sometimes in a wooden wagon that bounced along on the rutted road. I always wanted to help gather the Palo Verde for the stove that warmed the kitchen. Along the way were remains of bonfires that Grandpa built to burn the thorns from prickly pears, the winter forage for hungry cattle. We would see Jack Rabbits that scattered away faster than I now can gather my thoughts together.

September 2009

Night Rhymes With Fright

I toss in bed at midnight thinking of past years
of dreaming dreams, of hope, at times denying fears
there was no certainty to take away our doubt.
As for necessities, we had to do without.

A list would be too long, there were so many
but I could buy a candy cane if I had a penny.
A woman ate just carrots and turned a yellow shade.
It worried me. I wondered if her skin would fade.

We were kids, we didn't know the times were bad
we sensed that some days Mom and Dad were sad.
They laughed with friends and drank some wine
to take away the pain from struggles of the time.

So what am I to learn from this as I look back
to find that life has grays, not just white and black?
I want to be with others to work for what is right
to fight against the dark, to celebrate the light.

November 2005

Sit

Just sit comfortably on the chair
let my body go slack. Let my mind relax.
I'm not breathing.
I have to keep breathing. In. Out. In.
Out, ah, breath is good.
I need to breathe, can't forget that.

Body slack, mind at rest.
Why am I breathing so fast?
Why is the big toe on my left foot
sticking straight up?
Don't ask why, just breathe.
Oh, yes, let my breath
enter my toe, which toe?
The tight toe.
They're all tight.
All clenched up.
Except the big toe on my left foot.

What's that all about?
Don't question
just breathe in, and out.

Again.
That's better.
It's working.

Now breathe into my foot
breathe in, breathe out.

Why is my left foot sagging
as if it had no muscles?
Don't question, just breath
into my foot and out.

Look at me
all curled up in a ball.
I'm a tight ball of nerves
with flabby feet.

Breathe.
Take a breath
and assume an upright position.
In and out and up. Feel a string
reaching from my sit bones
up my spine through my head.
Feel myself dangling from the string.
Wow! This is good.

Oh, oh, I forgot to breathe.
Just breathe in. That's better.
Now breathe out.

January 2009

Waiting for Soon

Red sails in the sunset, far out on the sea
I would sing on my way to school.
I wondered about romance
could there be a ship out there
somewhere bringing love to me?

In those days, Daddy believed his ship
would come in, bringing gold
or news of a good job. Even on darkest days
he believed that just around the corner
there would be a rainbow.

Some live in the present, some live in the past
some sit on the shore and wait for a ship
which may be just beyond the sunset.
I have a long list of things to do today
I'll start right after I check the shipping news.

January 2010

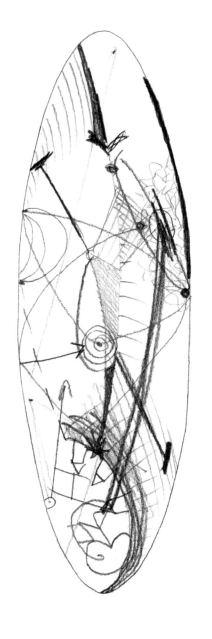

our dreams are like ships
that pass in the night
we live in different paradigms

Ships pass in the night, and speak to each other in passing, only a signal shown, and a distant voice in the darkness. So on the ocean of life, we pass and speak to one another, only a look and a voice, then darkness again and a silence.
~ Henry Wadsworth Longfellow

June, 2009

Finding Light

Cezanne had a way of seeing
through the light to life
as it is; no cows floating in the sky.
Light surrounds a bather, gives her form.
Light bounces off the peaches in a bowl.
The table sits squarely on the canvas.

Houses, hills and fields are there
just as he painted them. We imagine
where he sat to draw the cottage
on the corner, cows grazing
in the meadow. Light floats on the river
as it flows beneath the bridge.
At times it seems we also find the light.

February 2004

At Dawn

Red vapor trails pierce threatening clouds
and high above there is a spot of blue
where silly swirls like c's on a penmanship paper
make me think that sister has tapped
her ruler on the knuckles of an angel.

Three large sea birds fly along the cliff
alerting all to take notice while a chorus
of little birds begins to sing as light slowly
slips through a thin slit in a dark cloud.
Suddenly, the born again sun
paints a broad streak of orange
across gray water. In the western sky
the silver white moon begins to fade.

Celtics celebrated the changing light
this time of year. Later, the birth of Christ
the light of the world, was placed
in this dark season. Ancient peoples
worshipped the sun. Now as all of nature
announces its appearance I realize
it's awful glory. If it is impossible
to look in the face of the sun, know then
that the face of God is infinitely more blinding.

December 2010

there is a tie

a tie that binds us
your spirit and mine

a spirit that moves us
       when and how
             at the spirit's will

a tie that holds us
           tighter than gravity

the spirit will do as spirit wills

May 2008